SPARK
Unlock & Unblock Your Shine Potential

AJ SARCIONE
The Shine Scale™

©2019 Intivine, Inc.
All Rights Reserved

MAKING SUCCESSFUL PEOPLE **MORE SUCCESSFUL**

ACCELERATING SUCCESS

I've had some great success. I've worked with big brands and big leaders and made quick strides in my career. I believe that's because of my shine. My shine is made up of 14 different characteristics and attributes that come from the heart and mind. My goal is to help people understand personally how those traits work, and how they can be developed further, and that's why I created The Shine Scale™.

I want to help people make quicker strides to their success.

AJ SARCIONE

Shine Defined	9
Unintentional Perfection	17
Believe in Make Believe	23
Choose Positivity	37
Light & Bright	49
Each Day Be Better	63
Think Big Picture	77
Human Glitter	91
Building Others Builds You	103
Influencing Culture	115
Move Life Forward	125
Be Humble	135
Make It Count	147
Breaking Point	159
Care Less Not Careless	171
AgileAF	181
Get Sh*t Done	193
Write Your Story	205
Grow	217

SPARK

Shine Defined

You've Made A Spark

The power of possibility is within each of us. Some of us call it an ability to dream. Others say it's a focus of drive. Optimism is at the base of what we can be. When we doubt and allow insecurities and fear to take over, we underperform. Maybe you were a child whose parents never lifted you up. A teacher might have broken you down and another never helped you realize your potential. The friends you had may have impacted the opportunity you were given and you chose the wrong path.

Can you sing? If you said yes, I want to hear it. And if you can sing, I bet you can be better. If you said no, you're a liar. You aren't giving yourself the opportunity to make the universal language of music. You might not be Whitney Houston but you have control of your voice. You have control of the tone you can create. You are in control.

When you're done with this book you'll be that much stronger professionally and overall in how you are perceived in life. Not because you will have drastically changed. But because you will have broadened. And if you're open to it, you'll keep expanding. This will lead you to the belief that truly anything is possible. You must believe to achieve.

THIS BOOK WILL HELP

Am I some overly positive joker who doesn't realize life is hard and bullshit comes in all shapes and smells? Absolutely not. I'm real. I've learned you can always change the narrative. You write your story until you let someone else do it for you. So, if you feel like you've lost the pen, take the damn thing back! Grab the opportunity of your future, focus on it, write it. See yourself where you want to be and let it go. Let go of the worrying. Vision is most important. If you don't have one yet, you will. If you do, I expect it to grow.

This is about you. It's about two important parts of who you are. Your heart and your mind. Surely some of you are stronger in one area than the other. Maybe you think you are balanced, but are you using your heart and mind to their full potential? Once realized, you will achieve one of life's great faculties - the ability to shine. When you shine, wonderful things happen around you. It's what I like to call a state of unintentional perfection.

I'll give you this, if you're doing this work, and the flicker of what I hope to create for all of you dims, do me a favor. Take a break. But commit to relighting it. Commit to seeing the commitment through. It's a journey. One that needs to start now. So buck up, sit back, take this in, and I look forward to you finding the best version of you.

So, are you ready to make a spark? Well, you're reading this - let's do it!

INCREASE YOUR SHINE

WHAT IS SHINE?

Describe shine in your own words?

How does your heart play a role?

How does your mind play a role?

Aspects of you that are related more to your emotions and energy are connected to characteristics associated with your heart.

Characteristics that impact thought and focus are those associated more with the mind and go beyond intellect and concentrate on application.

When your heart and mind traits are fully engaged, you shine. Shining accelerates success. You radiate with a personality that is ignited by empathetic focus and strong emotional intelligence, creating an attraction to unintentional perfection.

When are moments you've felt your shine?

_____

What characteristics led to this?

_____

Have you taken
The Shine Scale™ yet?

THE SHINE SCALE™ RESULTS

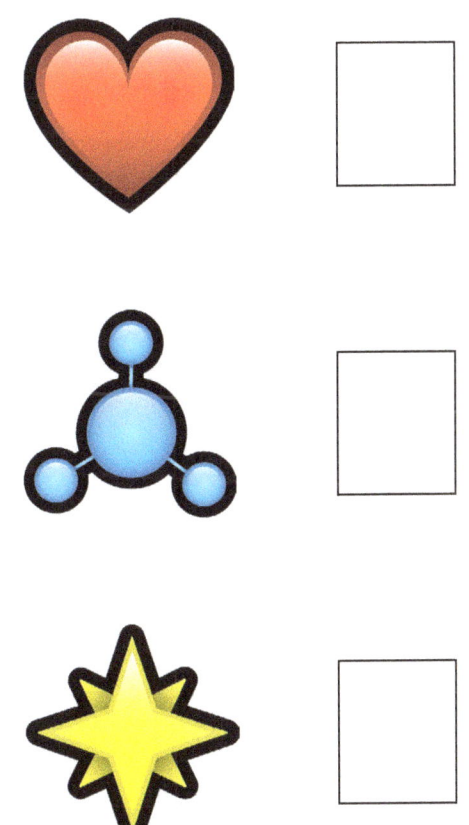

SPARK

Unintentional Perfection

GET UP GET UP GET UP
GET UP GET UP GET UP
GET UP GET UP GET UP
GET UP GET UP GET UP
GET UP GET UP GET UP
GET UP GET UP GET UP
GET UP GET UP GET UP
GET UP GET UP GET UP
GET UP GET UP GET UP
GET UP GET UP GET UP
GET UP GET UP GET UP
GET UP GET UP GET UP

UNITENTIONAL PERFECTION

Welcome each moment as another to build who you can become. These moments create a foundation for exactly who you'll be tomorrow. Moments that feel unintentionally perfect.

Heart, Mind, Shine. When your intellect is applied correctly with an empathetic focus, and your emotional quotient skills are high and you're in an optimistic state, you shine. People around you notice you more. Your impact grows and you grow with it.

For your mind, the importance is placed on specific attributes that are connected to how you apply your intellect and focus on empathy skills. For your heart, it's about how you emotionally approach a set of specific characteristics often related to energy. In combination, when these traits are engaged, they create a brightness called shine. You become someone who radiates something people desire. Doors open. Potential is met.

As the greatness comes to you, you begin to realize this moment is unintentionally perfect. I didn't construct this, I lived it. I didn't weasel my way into this, I welcomed the opportunity. I didn't worry about what was right, I focused on what was awesome. I had a sense that what was happening was meant to be and saw the beauty in it all. I focused on a future version of what I wanted to become. And I find reward in the mini-milestone of fulfillment I'm receiving today.

You can get unintentional perfection in your life when you engage your mind and heart potential to their greatest strengths, and thus shine. Because the shine you create propels you into the possibilities of what can become. And you're rewarded with growth and becoming a step closer to the vision for which you can't loose sight.

SPARK

Believe In Make Believe

What's your biggest dream?

_____

v   i   s   i   o   n (n)

the ablilty to think about or plan the future with imagination or wisdom

Do you have a vision in mind?

_____

VISION PLANNING

Close your eyes and picture a version of yourself

if money was free flowing, and every connection you needed was at your disposal

[DOODLE PAGE]

What holds you from pursuing your dreams?

_____

Do you believe that anything is possible?

_____

Yes, why? No, why?

_____

YOU HAVE TO BELIEVE TO ACHIEVE

—NANA

Who knows what
miracles
You can achieve
When you believe
somehow you will
You will when you
believe

I can prove it.

When I was a child, I dreamt of singing with Whitney Houston. How lucky would I be if I could actually sing with someone who I believe is one of the greatest singers of all time. How magical could life become if that were ever to be true.

The vision I had as a child was a foreshadowing to the future. Years later, while at a Whitney Houston concert, I was sitting in the front of the audience. This was my first time sitting in the front row at a show, and there's no other singer I would have begged my parents more to see this way than Whitney.

As she sang, I sang with her. I looked at her, we made eye contact, and it was as if our voices were singing along together. Then, she made her way over to me and the moment happened. Whitney quieted the audience and told them she wanted them to hear something. She walked toward me and extended her microphone. She told me to sing. And in an instant, my childhood dream came true. I was living my vision.

I believed in something so strongly that when the opportunity presented itself, the outcome came alive in the way I had always seen it.

<----- Those lyrics were sung by Whitney Houston in a song called "When You Beleive" written by Stephen Schwartz, featuring Mariah Carey, for the movie *The Prince of Egypt.*

List 5 words that describe how you feel
about where you're at in life today

-
-
-
-
-

List 5 words that describe where you'd
like to be in life today

-
-
-
-
-

challenge.

When you wish upon a star
Makes no difference who you are
Anything your heart desires
Will come to you

If your heart is in your dream
No request is too extreme
When you wish upon a star
As dreamers do
Fate is kind

Go and look in the mirror.
Read this to yourself.
Embrace the feeling.
Repeat.

"When you wish upon a star" written by Leigh Harline / Ned Washington
When You Wish Upon a Star lyrics © Bourne Co.

For ourselves, or for the teams we're a part of or lead, the power of possibility is unstoppable.

Believing in make believe opens your mind, and the minds you help guide, to unexpected outcomes. The limits we place will only result in a lack of opportunity. Your vision to see something greater and get those around you to see it too, will if nothing else, make one more door open.

[NOTES PAGE]

SPARK

Choose Positivity

GLASS HALF · GLASS HALF
EMPTY · FULL
CHOOSE POSITIVITY
GLASS HALF · GLASS HALF
FULL · EMPTY

Most say you can look at things in two ways: is the glass half full or half empty? Well, which is it?

Positivity is an integral aspect of shine. The energy you emit with positivity can be infectious.

It's all about perspective and how you look at life. Make it an opportunity, not a challenge. A challenge is negative. Yes, it's great to be challenged in life. But it's even greater to have an opportunity.

You might get some push back from those that are sour, but why let that break you down? It's the light you create with positivity that can help others see something from a different perspective.

don't fear success
YOU ARE AWESOME

What keeps you
from being happy?

_____

When are you
the most positive?

How does it feel to
be around positivity?

_____

_____

Who are some of the most
positive people in your life?

_____

p o s i t i v e (adj)

constructive, optimistic, or confident

[DOODLE PAGE]

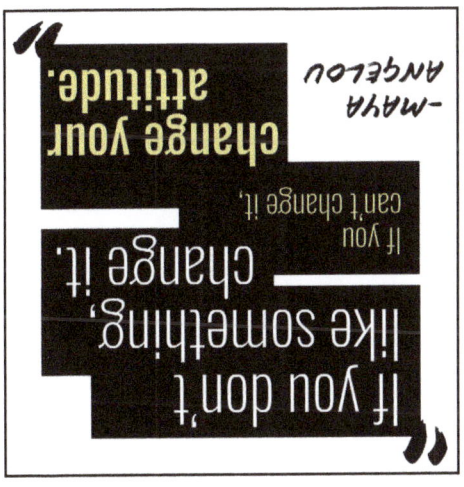

think.

You've arrived early to a meeting at work. The meeting is intended to find solutions to a creative problem you're facing with a new project.

Before the meeting starts, people are speaking negatively about the project you're about to discuss.

You can remain silent and do nothing. Or you can encourage them to change their perspective.

What's one thing you can do to change the energy?

How can you open their minds to focus more positively going into this meeting?

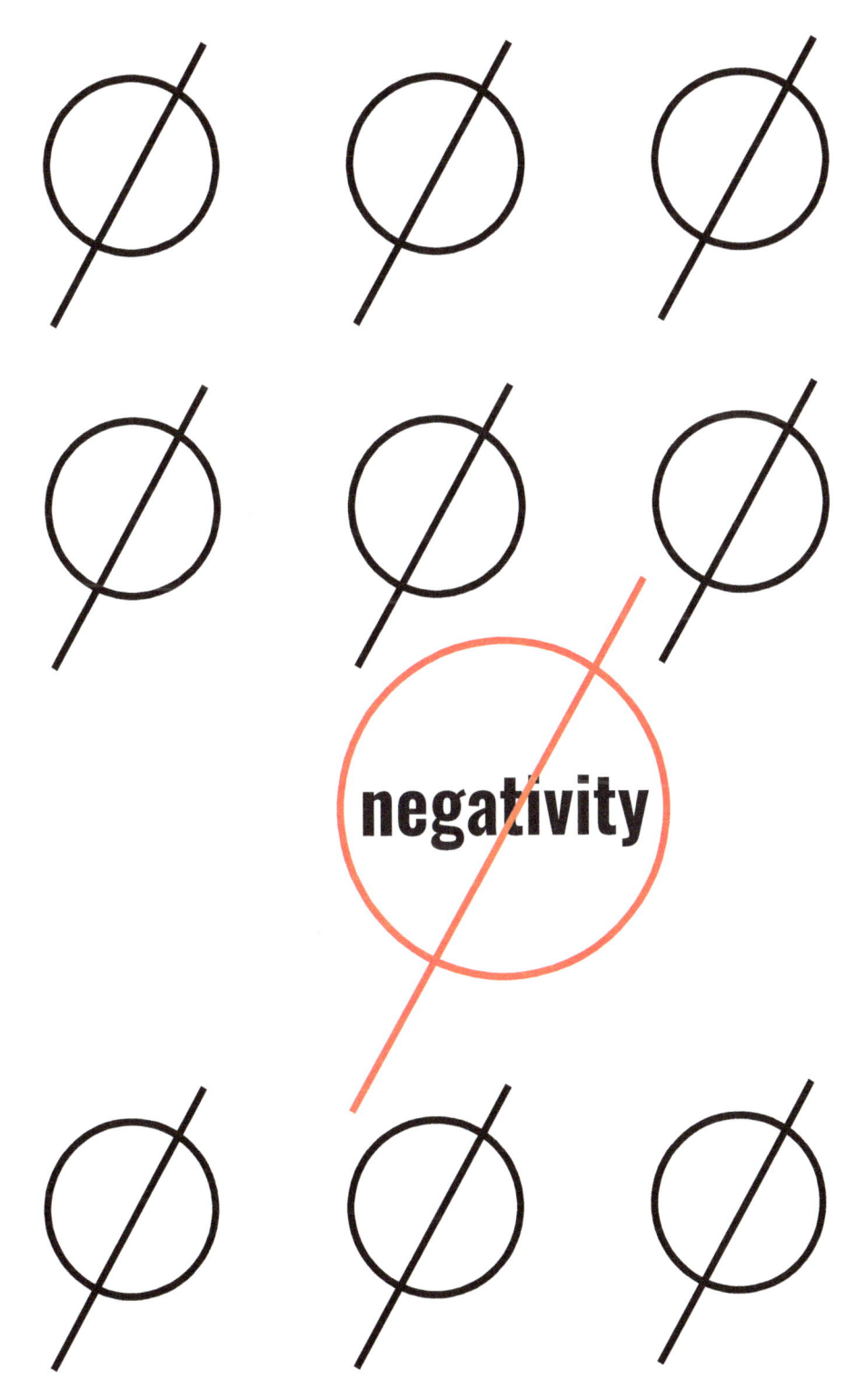

SPARK

Light & Bright

the moment before

Having control of our minds is crucial to how others perceive us. Like professional actors, we have an opportunity to check our minds and the way we're enterting a situation or conversation, as if we're waiting for a director to say "action." We have an ability to control our attitude, so when our energy is met by another person, it's not heavy.

How do you prepare yourself for a meeting?

_____

How do you know you'll do well during a speech?

_____

When people describe you, what would they say about your energy?

_____

Are you happy with that? Even if you are, what's one thing you could change?

_____

LIGHT
&
BRIGHT

The way we show up in a room in life or meeting at work can have a much greater impact on how people speak about us over time, well beyond the achievements for which we're known.

The energy that we create for ourselves and those around us is manageable, especially in times where we need a shift.

We have an ability to create how we show up. We can consciously allow ourselves to appear angry and disinterested. Or, we can walk into a room with a smile and willingness to be open to what we're about to encounter.

The energy we put into the space will impact the engergy we receive back from it and from those that are in it with us.

'Light & Bright' is a memorable approach to energy shifting.

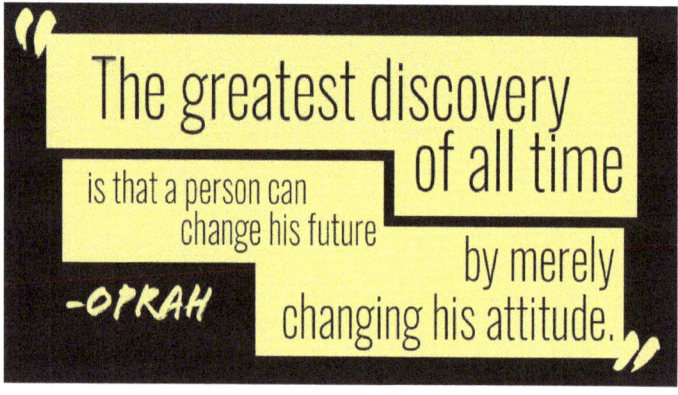

[NOTES PAGE]

b r i g h t (adj)

intelligent and quick-witted. giving off or reflecting a lot of light; shining

S H I N E

Do you feel that sometimes you are speaking because you feel the need to contribute? And if not, how do you feel about others who you think do this?

Out of insecurity, we often will want to participate to feel as though we have purpose and a place. But, if you have confidence and self awareness, others around you will see your value clearly over time.

[DOODLE PAGE]

3 takeaways for your next meeting

1) Show up with confidence. And even if you aren't delivering something you believe is your best, be proud and humble and welcome the constructive criticism.

2) Give yourself an opportunity to try a moment before if you need a reset.

3) When in doubt, remember light & bright, and you're likely to levitate a bit as you release the pressure.

SPARK

Each Day Be Better

T O D A Y
YOU ARE GREAT

T O M O R R O W
YOU ARE AMAZING

THE NEXT DAY
YOU ARE EXTRAODINARY

EACH DAY BE BETTER

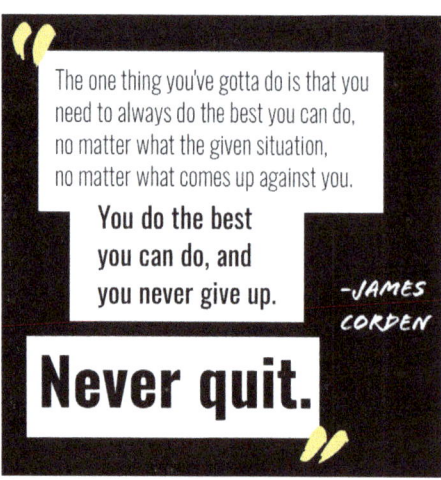

What did you not accomplish yesterday that you could do today?

_____

How do you hold yourself accountable?

_____

Define a goal you want to achieve by tomorrow.

_____

Hold yourself accountable to greatness.

Set small goals
When you do, know that even those might not always happen as planned.

Keep trying
When you fall off the horse (figuratively...and I suppose literally), get back on and ride a little faster than you were riding before. You will learn that set backs aren't meant to hold you back. They're meant to challenge you a bit more to make sure you have what it takes.

Help others
Be aware of people around you who need help and give it.

Manage your emotions
Know the energy you have and when you feel the wave of negative emotions coming, which you already know aren't worth it, calm them.

Creating positive daily habits can help us stay on the right track.

With a repetitive ritual we're able to find comfort in knowing we will complete something, which allows us to push for something greater.

How do you start your morning?

challenge.

Wake up 30 mintues earlier tomorrow than you did today.

Return here and share how you used the time.

EACH DAY BE BETTER

_____
_____
_____
_____
_____
_____
_____
_____
_____
_____
_____
_____
_____
_____

(Wait till tomrorow to move ahead.)
-----> kidding, you can keep going.

p e r s e v e r a n c e (n)

persistence regardless of how long or how hard
it is to achieve success

What has worked before to push yourself to something greater?

Example

- daily workouts

- video taping a practice or rehearsal

- seeking inspiration through books and quotes

You

_____

_____

_____

_____

_____

_____

_____

_____

_____

_____

AS   A

I WILL ... _____

TO   INSPIRE   THE
ME   TO   FOLLOW

& **LEADER**

_____

**PEOPLE   AROUND
IN   MY   SUCCESS**

SPARKS

Think Big Picture

THINK

BIG

PICTURE

Daydream

GO AHEAD, DO IT

ENJOY

A PUZZLE IS MUCH EASIER TO ASSEMBLE WHEN YOU HAVE THE FINAL IMAGE IN-FRONT OF YOU.

It's easy to get caught up in the day-to-day of life and loose sight of the bigger picture. We're often tasked with someting to do and accomplishing that takes precendece over focusing on why we might even being doing it in the first place.

Many leaders come to realize that what their driving towards is often found with many paths. Solving the puzzle doesn't always mean starting from a specific corner or finishing by putting the final middle piece in.

Thinking big picture means you're able to better pinpoint opportunities for getting to the final result. If you find you're not able to get that level of sight, step away. Take a vacation. Take a break. In that time, you naturally will return with a different perspective and insight - hopefully leading you to a place of greater understanding.

Do you find yourself focusing on the tactics and not the strategy?

_____

What keeps you from thinking big picture?

_____

If you remove what holds you back, what impact does it make?

_____

> "Five years from now I see myself still working hard to get where I want to be, because I think big."
>
> —CHANEL IMAN

THINK BIG PICTURE

When I think of my future, I find myself thinking about _____, which is _____ and full of _____.

I want to be able to find _____ and _____ which will make me feel like I am _____.

It will happen for me because I am _____ and with my ability to _____ and _____ I know I'm unstoppable.

Five years from now, I will _____ in a place that looks like _____ with people who are _____. I will have _____ and when I look in the mirror I will see _____ in my reflection.

WHEN YOU LOOK AT THIS IMAGE ----->
WHAT DO YOU SEE?

THINK BIG PICTURE

GR
AM

[NOTES PAGE]

DID YOU SEE THIS?

YOU ARE AS BIG AS YOU'RE WILLING TO LET YOURSELF BE. IF YOU EXPECT OTHERS TO SEE IT IN YOU, YOU HAVE TO SEE IT FIRST.

**I AM GREAT.
I AM AMAZING.
I AM EXTRAORDINARY.**

Human Glitter

EVEN IN A PITCH BLACK ROOM YOUR EYES WOULD SPARKLE

-my boarding school classmate

HUMAN GLITTER HUMAN
GLITTER HUMAN GLITTER
HUMAN GLITTER HUMAN
GLITTER **HUMAN GLITTER**
HUMAN GLITTER HUMAN
GLITTER HUMAN GLITTER
HUMAN GLITTER HUMAN
GLITTER HUMAN GLITTER

M O M

A RADIENCE, CAPTIVATING
OF JOY SO DESIREABLE
FINDING THE PERFECT CARD
WHERE TIME HAS NO STOPWATCH
FILLED WITH SPARKLES
ADORNED WITH COLOR ADHESED
FROM HER TO YOU
WITH A GUESS WHO?
MAKING SOMEONE FEEL SPECIAL
STARTS WITH SOMEONE SPECIAL
SPECIAL IS THE FEELING
WHEN SPECIAL IS IN THE HEART

FIND MEANING IN WHAT YOU GIVE, ALWAYS.

What have you done lately that made someone smile?

_____

What does sparkle mean to you?

_____

Do you ever think, how can I make somone's day better?

_____

challenge.

Once at a bar, the bartender was coming across angry and miserable. But, beyond her salty attitude, she had beautiful hair. In a moment of honesty, someone having a drink nearby gave her a compliment. And in an instant, a smile came over her. Her personality changed, and the drinks were poured a little better.

When you're in the presence of someone who is having a bad day, or woke up in the wrong way, give them a genuine compliment.

You'll spark them to shine.

We have the power to create change.
We have the option to share a compliment.
We have the ability to brighten someone's day.
We can make someone feel special.

You can be human glitter.

What's holding you back?

[NOTES PAGE]

PICK UP THE PHONE AND CALL SOMEONE YOU HAVEN'T IN A WHILE. DON'T WORRY ABOUT WHAT YOU'LL SAY. **ONLY BE READY TO SAY HI.** AND LET IT GO FROM THERE.

SPARK SPARK

Building Others Builds You

BUILDING OTHERS BUILDS YOU

BUILDING OTHERS BUILDS YOU

What does it mean to be a leader?

_____

How does it feel to positively impact another person's future?

_____

What does it mean to build?

_____

B U I L D

Seven months, thirteen different countries, cultures, and perspectives, all united by a new merger of different companies, with many people struggling to understand and embrace the future.

U n i t i n g everyone to see the potential in what could become of one united team that welcomes each other.

E n e r g i z i n g change for small improvements that appear as if they're too hard to achieve.

E d u c a t i n g

I n s p i r i n g

Building Is

- opportunity
- development
- encouragement
- support
- constructive criticsm
- reward
- repeat

Encourage people even when you fear their success might surpass yours. Your fuel could get them far and you could benefit from their success.

me

you

US

mentor (n)

someone with experience who is a trusted advisor

Do you have one? Why or why not?

_____

Are you one? Why or why not?

_____

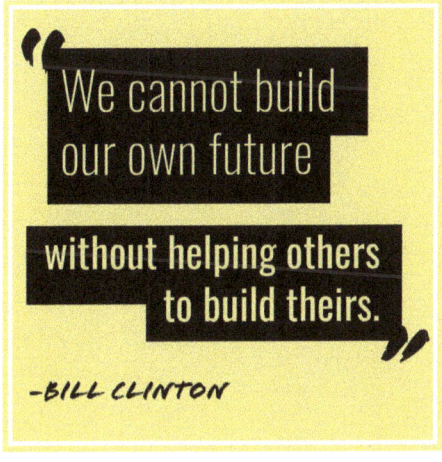

BE A
MOTIVATOR

Be somoene who can say:

People seek my opinon often. Even when my feedback is coarse and candid. They return because it's honest. And I mean well.

What will you do to help motivate those around you?

A spark is happening by you motiviating yourself to be better.

[DOODLE PAGE]

SPARK

06

Influencing
Culture

INFLUENCING
CULTURE

When you start a new job, how do the first few weeks feel?

_____

Have you ever welcomed someone new into your family who didn't fit in right at first?

_____

What does culture mean?

_____

OUR ABILITY TO IMPACT CULTURE

Listen. Observe. Respect. Live.

You must be a great listener. Active listening is key to participating in the growth of conversation. When you do, you'll observe and discover more clearly the world that's around you. We must all respect the differences of people and encourage them to respect it of others. Our differences can create friction, but the friction should move us forward positively and not be used against each other. Don't fear your heart. People will want to try and control you. Let yourself be seen and heard. Find people to go on the journey with you. What we accumulate in life is only as valuable as what it took to acquire it.

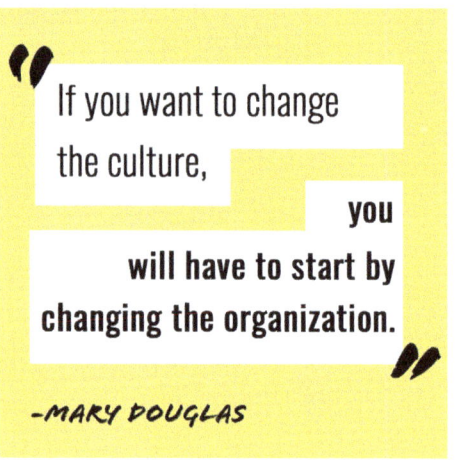

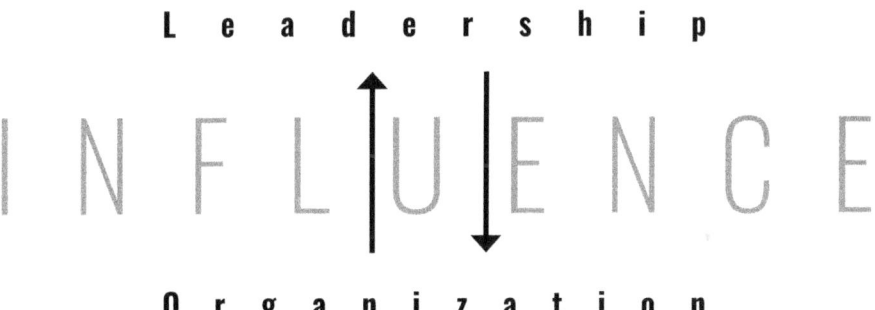

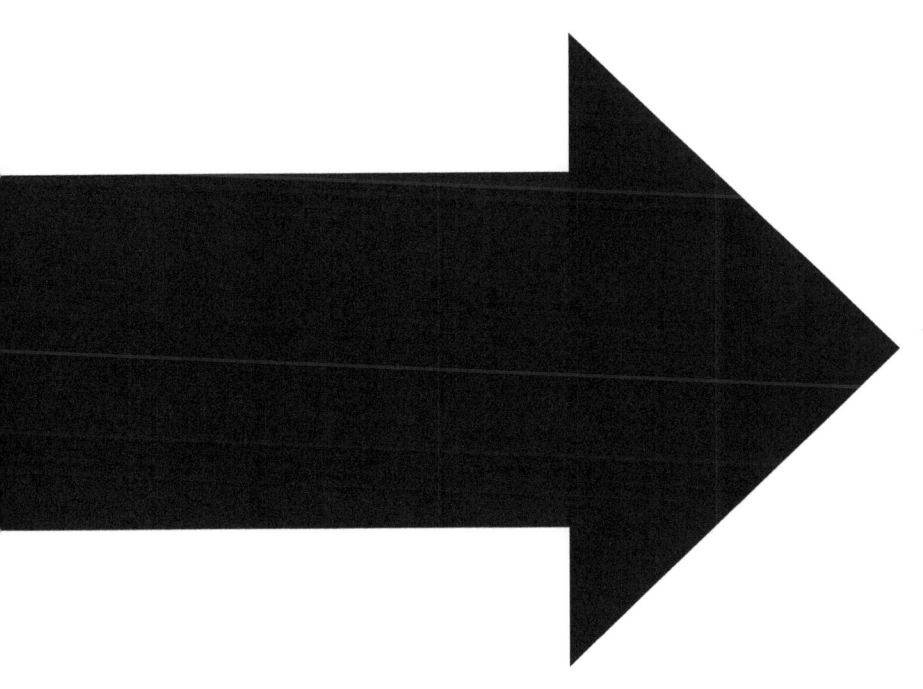

SPARKS

Move Life Forward

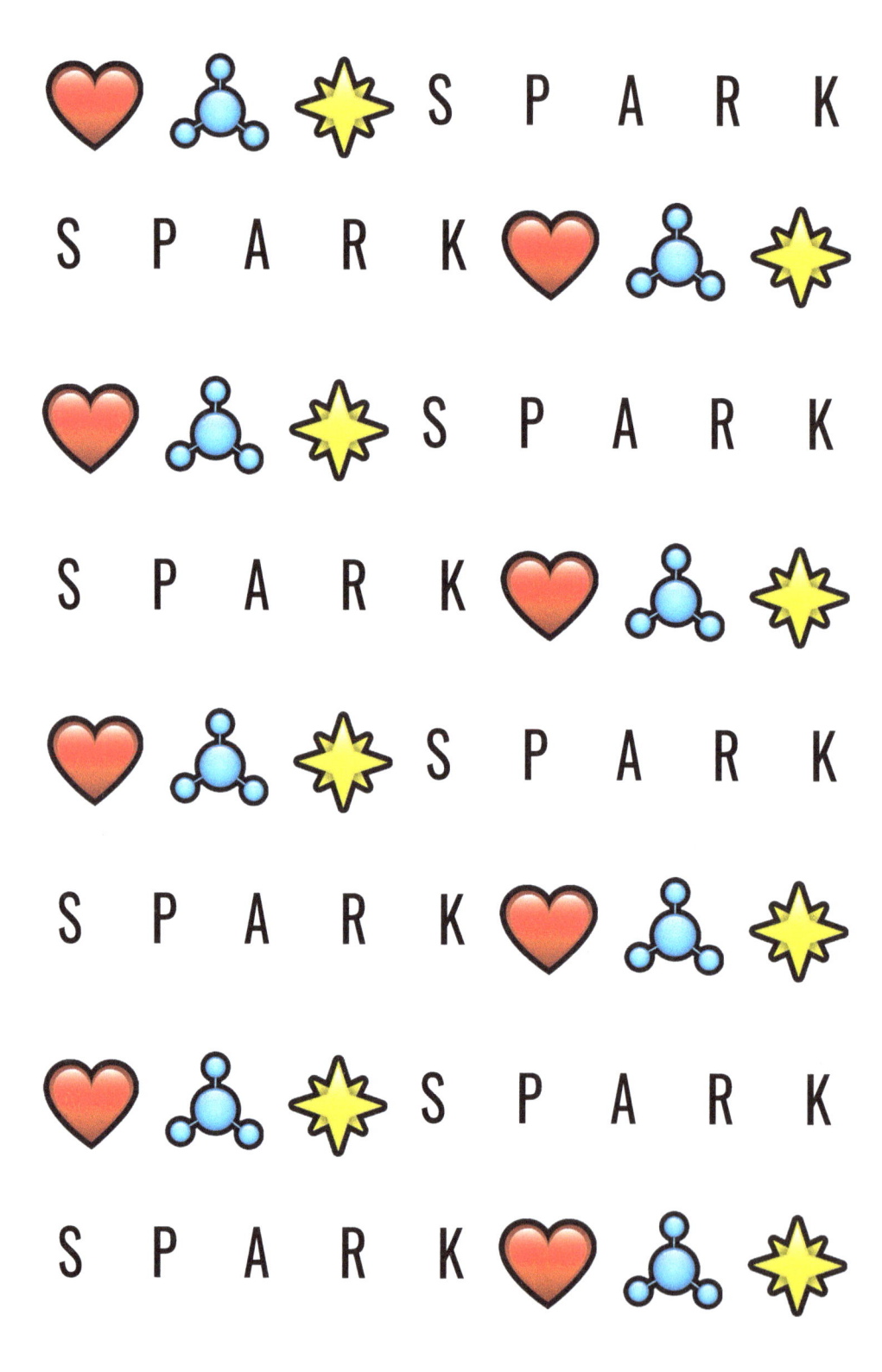

Sparks happen when we
make something happen.

STRUGGLE
&
STRIVE

We must engergize ourselsves to achieve something greater.

It's enevitable, what we plan for isn't what we always encounter. The approach shouldn't be to avoid these, but rather to be quick to see beyond them.

When a job change happens, or we realize a relationship we've built must take a shift from what we orginally had hoped for, we must not waste too much time belaboring the why after we've analyzed it, or we will loose potential for what is possible.

Having a mindset that you will overcome will lead you to something greater, always.

s   t   r   i   v   e (v)

to work hard for an achievement

What does it mean to strive:

_____

PICTURE A MOMENT IN YOUR
LIFE WHERE YOU STRUGGLED.
HOW DID YOU OVERCOME IT?

Do you ever look back and feel you haven't changed while others have?

_____

What does it feel like to move backwards in life?

_____

MOVE LIFE FORWARD

Future = Possiblity

Moving life foward starts with looking at your capabilities. Knowing what you're good at and what fuels you will help you open pathways to success.

Take leaps of faith and give yourself an opportunity to succeed. If you see the leap as a potential for failure, reset. You can win. Winning starts with a belief that you can, and you must try for it to happen.

Focus on your vision and what the next move can be towards achieving it.

Welcome the relationships you've made and don't be afraid to ask for help.

The past is behind you, the future is your possibility.

Invent it.

challenge.

Take action on
one thing you've
been holding back on.

Do it. Now.

(Another spark)

SPARK
SPA
BK

Be Humble

h u m i l i t y (n)

state of being humble; free from arrogance with a modest opinion of self importance

BE HUMBLE
BE HUMBLE
BE HUMBLE
BE HUMBLE
BE HUMBLE
BE HUMBLE
BE HUMBLE
BE HUMBLE

Do you feel lucky?

_____

What grounds you?

_____

What do you expect in life?

_____

EXPECTATIONS

We often find disapointment when our expecations ask too much of other people or of the situations we're in.

When we want people to be someone they previously haven't been, how can we be disappointed. If an environment has proven to be a certain way, and we enter into it believeing it will be different, how can we think anything will be new from what it was before?

Once we know and understand the traits of people around us, let those traits influence and set your expectations. This doesn't discount your ability to try and create change. Try and try again. But, as you do, be clear what your lowest common denominator is, so anything you're able to influence is a reward and not something you're expecting.

You expected the writing on this page to be the other way. Well, deal with it. It's like this.

EXPECTATIONS

Similar to aligning on better expectations, other areas of focus help us to be humble. It's important to remember that what we gain can go way. So we must not take advantage of our achievements. An important component of this is not being arrogant. When we welcome others' opinions and thoughts, and understand our value is all the same regardless of titles or wealth, better relationships are built. And as we've discussed, through those, building of each other can net out in amazing outcomes.

It's important to know where you came from and what you've created and who helped you get there. Have a sense of roots. Trees in a forest don't all grow tall to the sky or grow wide and create cover for other plants to grow, or create maple syrup, or a place for a bird to nest. But, they all start with a root. A precious anchor that when ruined not much can grow from it.

Be humble.

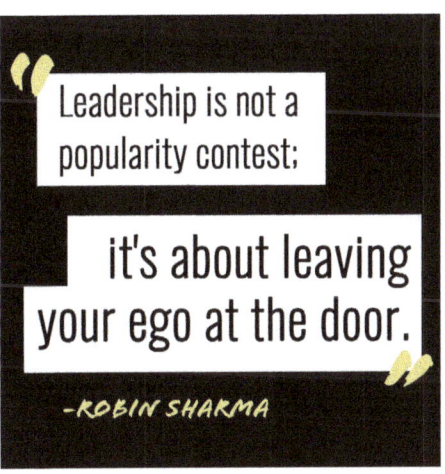

Brilliant leaders are created beyond their intellect and resumes. The leaders who shine are those that welcome the opinions of others around them, and showcase a level of accessbility while not dimishing their position of knowledge and responsibility.

What was your childhood like?

What have you created in life?

Who helped you get to your success?

challenge.

Send that person,
or persons,
that you just described,
a quick note
to say thank you.

Yes, right now.

[NOTES PAGE]

[maybe jot down the responses you receive]

SPARK

Make It Count

multitasking (v)

to perform more than one activity at the same time

MAKE IT COUNT   MAKE IT
COUNT   MAKE IT COUNT
MAKE IT COUNT   MAKE IT
COUNT   **MAKE IT COUNT**
MAKE IT COUNT   MAKE IT
COUNT   MAKE IT COUNT
MAKE IT COUNT   MAKE IT
COUNT   MAKE IT COUNT

Do you believe everything has a reason?

_____

Do you accept and make the most of everything you're faced with?

_____

What matters most to you in life?

_____

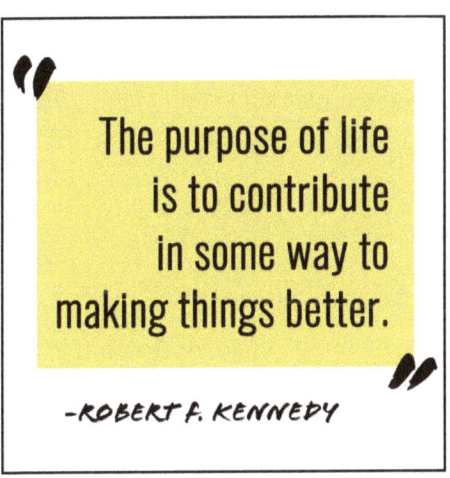

F O C U S

Look inside yourself and find what the meaning of your existence is and live for it.

As you do, put your electronics away. Listen and take in human experiences that are present around you.

Don't talk to hear yourself speak. Choose to participate when you have something worthwhile to contribute.

Be prepared. Know the outcome desired before you enter into a situation. Your result will be stronger and more aligned with what makes you feel satisfied.

What does it mean to listen to someone?

_____

How often do you find yourself on your phone and not in the conversation?

_____

When is the last time you recognized you weren't present? Why?

_____

FOCUS
PRESENCE

GREATER REWARD

challenge.

Next meeting,
put your phone
and your computer
away.

Bring a notepad.
Take notes.
With a pen.

Breaking Point

You were my breaking point.
The strength that I need.
You were my breaking point.
The pain from what I feed.
Without you, where would I be.
For that I can thank you.
You were my breaking point.
Now I'm taking control of me.

BREAK
BREAKING
POINT
THROUGH

Even when it seems like everything is going in the right direction, it's enevitable something will arise that creates conflict. As we move life forward, there can be moments where so much is being asked of us that we don't see the reality of what we're facing, and we must clear our heads in order to open up and see what's waiting for us on the other side.

Moments of challenge are moments of opportunity.

BE KIND   TO

YOURSELF

IN MOMENTS OF

DEVELOPMENT

When was the last time you had a breakthrough?

_____

What has been an obstacle in your life?

_____

Has there been something in your past that was hard to handle? Was the experience worth it?

_____

~~CHALLENGE~~
OPPORTUNITY

[DOODLE PAGE]

PERSEVERANCE

Don't accept defeat.

You may find a time where it seems like everything you've worked for is crumbling. And that there is no positive potential ahead of you. But, if you allow that to be true, you're giving in to what it is that is breaking you, and not allow you to break through it.

Focus on your vision and the next milestone you want to meet. Don't lose yourself and what matters to you most by the conflict you face.

There will always be many lenses you can look through. But, you must choose the one that sees a positve potenital for growth.

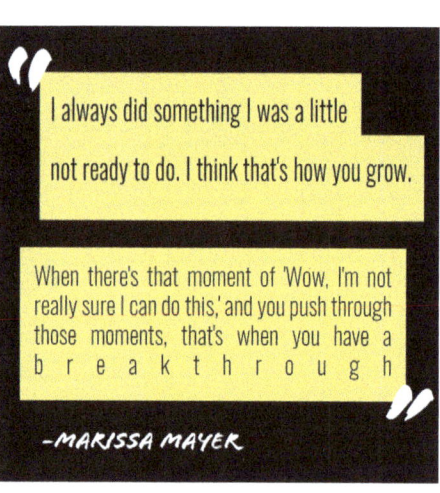

[NOTES PAGE]

Care Less
Not Careless

l   o   v   e (n)

a strong feeling of affection

h   a   t   e (n)

an intense feeling of dislike

i   n   d   i   f   f   e   r   e   n   c   e (n)

without feeling of interest or concern

CARE LESS not CARELESS

THE OVERACHIEVER

It's all about managaing your expectations.

There have to be lines drawn to avoid burnout and burning bridges. As an overachiever, success will often come abundantly, but at what cost? The drive and desire to win or accomplish shouldn't be discouraged. But the approach we take to what we believe is requried of us must be carefully developed.

As a leader, it's healthy for people to see you as a go-getter. But they must also see someone who has balance and respect, level-headedness and acceptance.

Rationalize better what it is you're working toward so you're able to worry less and enjoy it more.

LOOSE 'EM or SET 'EM

EXPECTATIONS
EXPECTATIONS
EXPECTATIONS
EXPECTATIONS
EXPECTATIONS
EXPECTATIONS
EXPECTATIONS

Have you ever spent too much time worrying about what never even happened?

_____

Do you think things will fall in to place no matter what?

_____

What makes you anxious?

_____

SPARK

COVER. OUR. COLLECTIVE. ASSES.

Checks & Balances

Originally acquired many years ago while working in an agency setting, this concept is meant to help create protection by thinking ahead.

As a team, we must work together to support what is greater than our own individual task. Sometimes the implication of carelessness on one person's part will have a huge affect on many others involved. So, we have to all work towards ensuring what we do will help to prepare us for the best possible outcome.

That might mean making sure the right people are included in an email, or that we limit the amount of opportunity for someone to poke holes into a project by sharing details ahead of time, or being transparent.

This is helpful when you're looking to manage the amount of stress you might be creating. Part of that management is finding ways to reduce an overachieving expectation, by making sure at the end of it all we as a team are covered. You can then find comfort in your approach more easily.

Agile AF

I am able. can. will.
I am able. can. will.
I am able. can. will.

#agileAF

as f*ck

AGILE AF

You are capable.

If you can welcome what comes your way and believe that you will find success, at the least, you'll do the best you can.

This crazy world of work and life is really a game of people trying to figure something out and hoping for the best. If you can realize you're part of that game, you winning is as simple as making it past jail or getting past go.

What can help us most are tools that protect and propel us. These can be acquired or developed, but it's important to think of them in times of uncertainty. They can help to make something unfamiliar more famliar, if you're able to look at a new task in a way that can seem recognizable. By seeing common denominators in the work, or finding a way to rationalize getting someting done in a way that you're used to, you can achieve an outcome.

Do the best you can.

How often do you say no and why?

_____

How do you feel when the tides change and you're faced with unexpected headwinds?

_____

If you could go back in time and go to school again, what would you study?

_____

During an orientation for a big tech company, I led a conversation about welcoming opportunities that come with working for a large, global brand. People were encouraged to be open to what might come to them and be willing to accept that the job they were joining with might not be the one they would be in next year or in the years to come. One of the new hires embraced this idea and a few months after joining, reached out to me to let me know the impact that it was having on her. She had originally joined to support a VP, and after a few months, with an open mind and willingness to take on what came her way, she found herself interviewing to support the CEO; ulimatley becoming one of the most important people in the company, only a few months after she started.

Welcome opportunities and know you will succeed.

> Your ability to figure something out is only limited by your belief that you're not capable.

HAVE FUN

Dream Team

A group of people having fun. Building something together, with daily changes and pivots unexpectedly.

Growing together, making a difference.

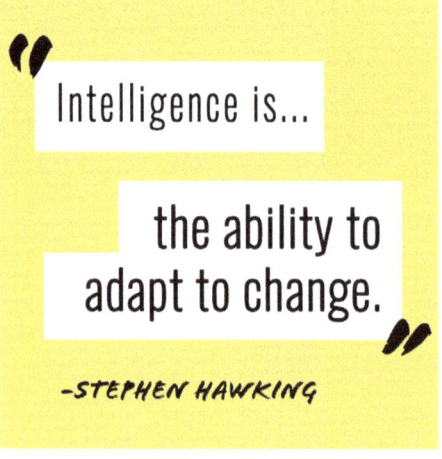

[DOODLE PAGE]

SPARK SPA
BK

Get Sh*t Done

G E T

D O

SH*T
NE

T Building tools to help capture information or allow creativity to flow can be highly effective with getting work completed.

O The briefing process in a campaign is one of the most important steps as it helps to aggregate and provide information that allows designers to create.

O Project managers leverage programs and processes to help ensure work is done right and done on time.

If you're new to leading a team or looking to drive results more strongly, turn to tools.

L If you're seeking to help others to be more effective in their outputs, turn to tools.

Tables and forms that request thought to help drive putting an idea and insight to paper. Mechanisms to unstick.

S **Tools will help unlock potential and get results.**

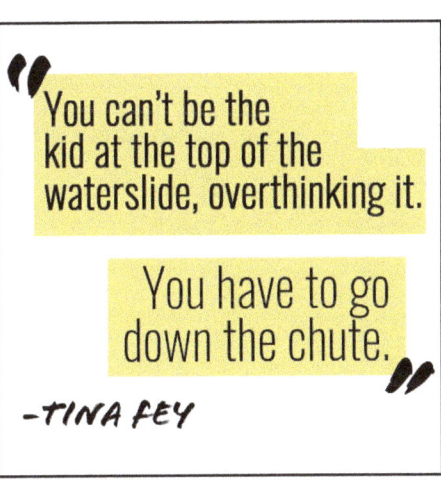

CAPABLE
PROGRESSION
DEDICATION

R E S U L T S

The juggler

Are you ever amazed by some people's ability to do it all. A friend who is a parent, working an important job, while taking care of an elderly relative, and building a side hussle, yet somehow never seems to miss your birthday. They get shit done.

It's easy to feel overwhelmed if you focus on too many things at once, but part of the success of getting things done is being able to allow all of those to exist amongst each other, focusing on what's important in the moment and being able to pivot and come back to whatever it is you were focused on before.

When you spend too much time worrying about what it will take or how you'll do it verses putting energy into figuring out the how and living through it, you're wasting time.

tip.

You might be asked to travel a lot for work and rather than focusing on how the time change might affect you, go to sleep as you normally would and wake up with the morning light. It helps reset you.

Use light to help you avoid jetlag.

BE AHEAD OF THOSE FROM WHOM YOU SEEK APPROVAL

What are you most
passionate about?

What usually holds you
up from getting work done?

What's your go to
procrastination activity?

What does it feel like
to complete something?

[NOTES PAGE]

SPARK

Write Your Story

YOU'VE Spark MADE A SPARK

WRITE YOUR STORY

Shining comes from within.
You be the author
of how you're seen.

N A R R A T I V E

Be your own PR person

Clothes and your surroundings dictate something about who you are.

The world will not always perceive correctly what your intentions are, so you must be aware and realize that your image is more than how you look.

The words and the ways you use them, and your energy and how you recieve others, among other things, will create the story people tell about you.

Determine what you want to be remembered for and live by it.

Find what you love, do what you love, and what you love will give you a life you love

When there are moments in your life where you feel overwhelmed, embrace them. Take time to refuel and come back with a bang. What's waiting for you will require more energy and a stronger mindset, so allow yourself the opportunity to revive and prepare.

[NOTES PAGE]

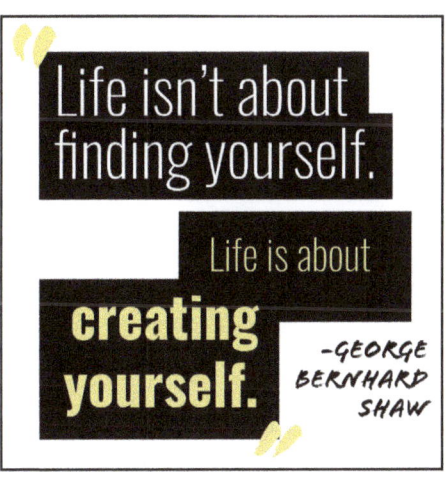

You finishing this book.
S P A R K ♥ ⚛ ✨

You applying this work.
S P A R K ♥ ⚛ ✨

You digging depper to discover more.
S P A R K ♥ ⚛ ✨

challenge.

Apply this thinking
and concepts
to how you approach
life and work.

Take The Shine Scale™ again.

SPARK

Grow

IF YOU THINK YOU'RE DONE, YOU'VE ONLY JUST BEGUN

A person who shines knows that there is always more to do.

There's always something new to conquer.

Improvements in yourself should be discovered frequently and throughout life.

What you've achieved here is the start of what you'll gain in years to come if you're willing to grow.

Putting these concepts at the front of your mind today will help them become something that triggers sparks tomorrow.

When you revist The Shine Scale™ in the future, an increase in your heart, mind and shine is the goal.

A new speed to what you can achieve begins now.

Spark. Shine. Accelerate your success.

THE SHINE SCALE™ RESULTS

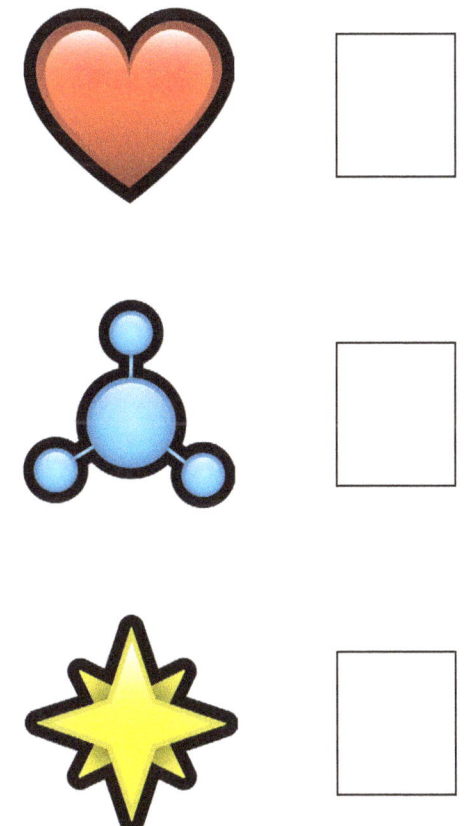

THE SHINE SCALE™

GET YOUR SHINE.COM

www.ingramcontent.com/pod-product-compliance
Lightning Source LLC
Chambersburg PA
CBHW062026290426
44108CB00025B/2795